ABC'S OF ECOLOGY

Isaac Asimov

WALKER AND COMPANY

New York

ACKNOWLEDGMENTS

A. W. Ambler from National Audubon Society, pp. 24 (day lily), 28.

The American Museum of Natural History, pp. 24 (lion), 29 (mimicry).

Arizona Tourist Bureau, p. 44.

Anita Benarde, p. 4.

Mark Boulton from National Audubon Society, p. 41 (right).

Walter Dawn from National Audubon Society, p. 5.

Environmental Protection Agency, Office of Public Affairs, p. 13.

Fairchild Aerial Surveys, Environmental Protection Agency, p. 37.

Fleischman Laboratories, Standard Brands, Inc., p. 46.

John H. Gerard from National Audubon Society, pp. 6, 24, 45.

Georgia Pacific Paper Division, p. 47.

Ron Jannis, Mayor's Council on the Environment, p. 35.

Joint Task Force One, p. 14.

Maurice and Sally Landre from National Audubon Society, p. 23.

Victor Lopez, Environmental Protection Administration, p. 30 (overpopulation).

C. G. Maxwell from National Audubon Society, p. 39.

The New York Times, p. 8.

Irvin L. Oakes from National Audubon Society, p. 42.

Research Laboratories, General Motors Corporation, p. 33.

Leonard Lee Rue III from National Audubon Society, pp. 30, 48 (left).

United Nations, pp. 12, 17, 31.

United States Atomic Energy Commission, p. 34.

United States Department of Agriculture, Office of Information, pp. 20, 38 (inset).

United States Department of Agriculture, Soil Conservation Service, pp. 7, 9, 11, 16, 18, 19, 27, 29, 32, 38 (top), 40, 41 (left), 48 (right).

Wide World Photos, pp. 10, 36, 43.

First published in the United States of America in 1972 by the Walker Publishing Company, Inc.

Published simultaneously in Canada by Fitzhenry & Whiteside, Limited, Toronto.

Trade ISBN: 0-8027-6098-8
Reinf. ISBN: 0-8027-6099-6
Library of Congress Catalog Card Number: 77-186174

Printed in the United States of America.

Designed by Lena Fong Hor

To Millie and Margery

A is for Additive,

_____

_____

_____

a material added for improvement. Additives might give food a nicer color, a better taste, or more nutrition. They might make the food keep better. Sometimes additives can harm the body. It is important to study additives closely to make sure they are not harmful.

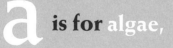 **is for** algae,

_____

_____

_____

simple water plants without roots, stems, and leaves.
Some algae look green or blue-green, while others look
brown or red. Algae include microscopic single-celled
plants as well as giant-sized seaweeds. They serve as
food for many animals that live in the sea.

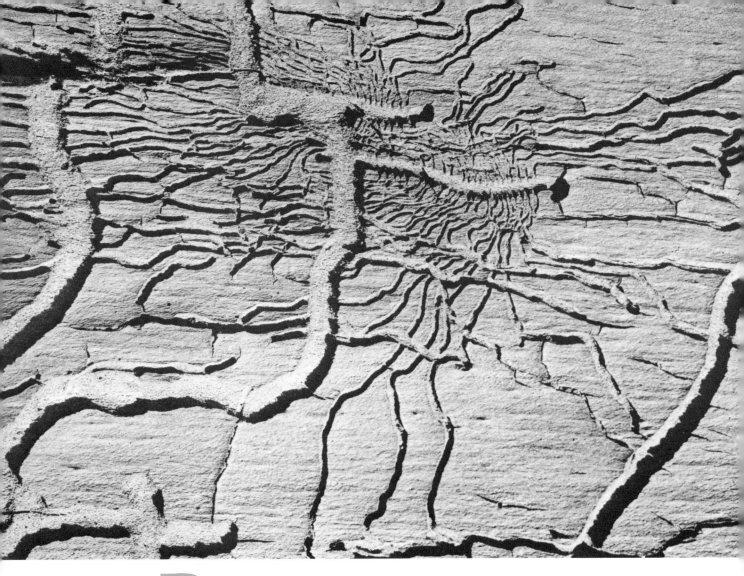

B is for Bark beetle,

_____

_____

_____

a small insect that tunnels under the bark of trees.
When too many of them are under the bark, they may
kill the tree. Some types spread disease from one
tree to another. The Dutch elm disease, which has
killed many elm trees, is spread by bark beetles. This
is an example of how a small insect can upset the
balance of nature.

Woodland biome

b is for biome,

_____

_____

_____

a large part of the earth that has the same kind of
climate. The climate makes conditions good for certain
plants. These plants, in turn, provide food and shelter
for certain kinds of animals. A large northern evergreen
forest is an example of a biome. So is a wide flat
grassland. Even a city can make up a biome in which
certain plants and animals live.

7

C is for Carbon monoxide,

_____

_____

_____

a colorless, odorless gas that is produced when fuel
isn't burned completely. It is very poisonous even in
small amounts. Coal fires can make people dizzy and ill
if there is no way for fresh air to get into the house.
Automobiles produce carbon monoxide. Too many
cars bring about air pollution.

C is for conservation.

_____

_____

_____

the ways in which people can act to keep from using up or spoiling the natural resources of the earth. We can learn to preserve our forests, fish, wildlife, soil, minerals, and water. For example, plans can be made to replace the trees cut down in the forest for lumber. We can prevent over-fishing so that some fish will be left in the sea to lay eggs for future generations.

D is for Detergent,

_____

_____

_____

a chemical that helps mix oil and water. It is used to clean oily dirt from clothes. If too much gets into lakes and rivers, it can change the balance of nature. Useful bacteria and organisms are killed and water is filled with suds and lather.

d is for drought,

_____

_____

_____

less rain than usual for a long period of time. When this happens, the water level sinks in wells, rivers, and lakes. The ground is dryer and plants do not grow. If drought continues for too long in a region and plants die, no food remains for animals and people.

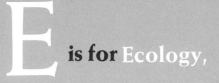

E **is for Ecology,**

_____

_____

_____

the study of the way in which living things act on each other and their surroundings and the way their surroundings affect them. Today people must study ecology to find out how to keep from spoiling the lakes, rivers, oceans, land, and air of the earth they live on.

Official symbol for the United Nations Conference on the Human Environment

e is for eutrophication,

_____

_____

_____

the heavy growth of algae and bacteria in a pond or lake into which wastes are poured. The chemicals in the waste provide food for the algae and bacteria which multiply. When the algae and bacteria die, they decay and use up the oxygen in the water. As a result, many other animals, such as water insects and fish die. The lake becomes choked up with dying plants and animals.

F is for Fallout,

the slow dropping to earth of dangerous radioactive particles after an atomic bomb has exploded. The tiny particles are blown high into the air and only come down little by little over a period of years. Because of fallout, the United States does not test atom bombs above ground anymore. Nuclear power plants have to have built-in safety equipment installed to prevent accidents.

An atomic bomb explosion

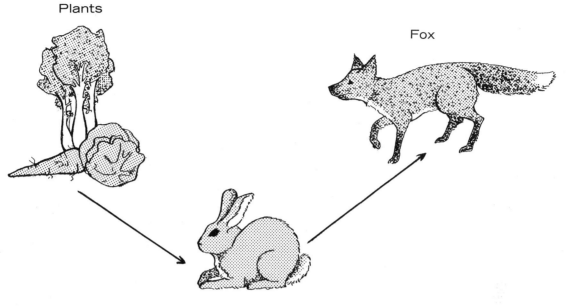

Plants

Fox

Rabbit

FOOD CHAIN

f **is for** food chain,

where one life form is eaten by another, which is eaten
by another, which is eaten by another and so on.
Plants are eaten by a rabbit, which is eaten by a fox.
This is an example of a short food chain. The higher up
a food chain an animal is, the fewer there can be.
There are fewer foxes than rabbits.

15

G is for Game refuge,

_____

_____

_____

an area set aside for animal and plant life. There is no hunting or fishing allowed, so that the wildlife can live their natural lives in peace. Men can study ecology and animal behavior in such places and learn useful facts about nature. In Africa, some game refuges are thousands of square miles in size.

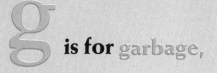

g **is for** garbage,

_____

_____

waste produced by man. Most of it is leftover food.

More and more garbage is produced each year. People

try to find good uses for it. Some garbage can be used

to fill up large holes in the ground. If garbage is treated

and pressed down hard, it can even be made into

building materials.

HUMUS

H is for Humus,

_____

_____

_____

plant and animal matter that was once living but has died and decayed. Humus often covers a forest floor and can be very useful. It is spongy and holds water, so plants can grow better. It also helps supply minerals to the soil. Humus is food for some animals such as earthworms and some plants such as mushrooms.

h **is for** herbivore,

————————————————————
————————————————————
————————————————————

any animal that eats plants. Cattle and sheep are
herbivores. So are rabbits and squirrels, deer and
antelope. There are also animals that eat other animals.
Such animals are carnivores. Lions and tigers are
carnivores. So are weasels and owls. Most sea animals
are also carnivores.

I is for Insecticide,

_____
_____
_____

a chemical that kills insects. DDT is the most
well-known insecticide. It is important to kill some kinds
of insects that eat crops and carry disease. But DDT
also can harm other kinds of animals. For example, in
a food chain, each animal absorbs the poisons of its
prey. The simple water plants in a river may have a
small amount of DDT but the worms that feed on them
will have a greater amount of DDT and the fish that
eat the worms will have a still greater amount.

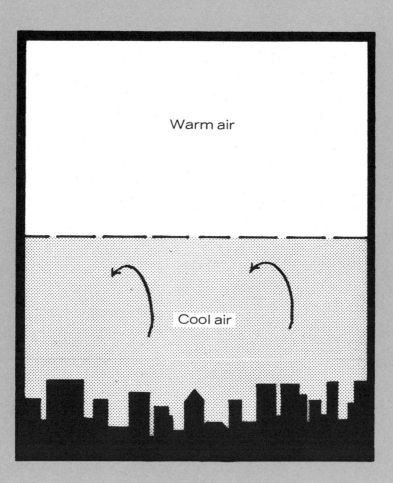

Warm air

Cool air

INVERSION

i **is for inversion,**

_____

_____

_____

when the upper air is warmer than the lower air. When
this happens, there is no wind and the lower air doesn't
move. It may stay over a city for days and get full of
smoke particles and dust. Pollution levels are then high
and the lungs can be harmed.

21

J is for Juvenile water,

_____

_____

_____

water that appears on the surface of the earth for the first time. When the earth was first formed, water was trapped deep underground. Volcanoes emit clouds of water vapor from this underground source. This water then stays on the surface of the earth and is used by living things.

Volcano emitting steam

j is for junk,

_____

_____

_____

solid waste that is hard to get rid of or to put to use again. Plastic and metal objects are examples. They don't decay and just pile up. As there are more and more people who use more and more things, there is more and more junk. It is very hard to find places to put junk and keep it out of the way. We have to learn new ways to put junk to use.

K is for Key industry animals,

those which are so numerous and widespread that they are important food for other animals. They are the beginning of an animal food chain because they feed on plants. In the ocean, tiny shellfish are key industry animals that live on floating algae. In meadows, mice are key industry animals.

A day lily is a member of the plant kingdom

A lion is a member of the animal kingdom

k **is for** kingdom,

the broadest division of living things. There are two
kingdoms—plant and animal. Plants are rooted in the
ground or float on the sea and make use of the energy
of sunlight. Animals move about and get their energy
by eating other living things. Tiny one-celled creatures
are sometimes put in one or the other of these kingdoms.

25

Eggs

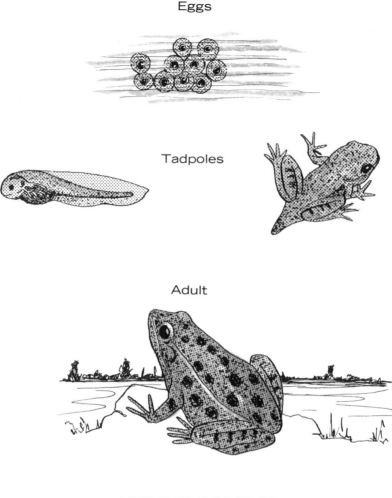

Tadpoles

Adult

LIFE CYCLE OF FROG

L is for Life cycle,

_____

_____

_____

the changes through which a living thing passes from
the time it is born to when it dies. A frog, for instance,
begins as an egg. This hatches into a tadpole with a tail
but no legs. The tadpole develops legs, loses its tail
and becomes a frog. The frog gets bigger and older and
finally dies.

26

Oxygen was the limiting factor here

l is for limiting factor,

_____

_____

_____

anything in the surroundings of a living thing that keeps
it from increasing in numbers to more than a certain
amount. There may not be enough food or oxygen to let
it increase in numbers further, or enough water. Or
disease may develop, or other animals that feed on it
may become more numerous.

M is for Mutualism,

the way in which two different living things can cooperate. The great sea anemone has stinging tentacles that can kill fish. But the clown fish lives among these same tentacles and is not stung. Some of the food the clown fish catches goes to the anemone. The clown fish also cleans the anemone's tentacles. In return, it is provided with shelter.

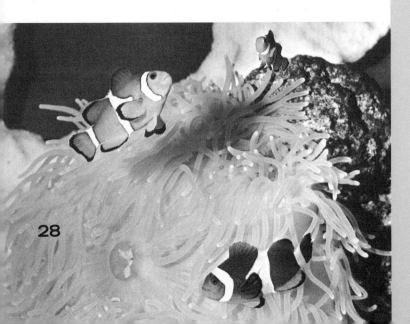

m is for mimicry,

the way in which one life form imitates another. There are some butterflies that taste bad to birds and are hardly ever eaten. Other butterflies that taste good happen to have wing patterns just like the bad-tasting ones. Birds leave the imitators alone, too. So the edible species escapes death because it resembles the inedible one. An example is the Viceroy butterfly, which mimics the Monarch butterfly.

Monarch butterfly

Viceroy butterfly

N is for Nitrogen cycle,

the passing of nitrogen atoms from one place to another. Bacteria change nitrogen in air to nitrogen compounds in soil. Plants absorb the compounds and change them to protein. Animals eat the plants and change them into animal protein. When plants or animals die, nitrogen compounds from the proteins enter the soil. These break down. Nitrogen enters the air and it all starts over again.

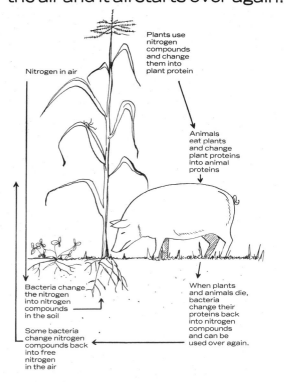

Nitrogen in air

Plants use nitrogen compounds and change them into plant protein

Animals eat plants and change plant proteins into animal proteins

Bacteria change the nitrogen into nitrogen compounds in the soil

Some bacteria change nitrogen compounds back into free nitrogen in the air

When plants and animals die, bacteria change their proteins back into nitrogen compounds and can be used over again.

NITROGEN CYCLE

n is for natural resources,

all the things in the world used by living things. There is the water supply, the food supply, and the supply of clean air. There are coal and oil fuels to burn for energy and there are minerals to use in manufacturing. Natural resources can get used up. We must be careful not to waste them and to replace them when they are used up.

O is for Overpopulation,

_____

_____

_____

the increase in numbers of animals or plants to where there is not enough food or water or space for them. When animals or plants become overpopulated, some of them may starve or die of sickness. Then the numbers go down again. Right now, some people think that our world will soon be overpopulated with human beings.

O is for omnivorous,

_____

_____

_____

the ability to eat both plant and animal life. Animals that are omnivorous can often get along very well because they don't have to stick to one kind of food. They are less likely to starve. Rats and bears are examples of omnivorous animals. So are pigs and men.

P is for Pollution,

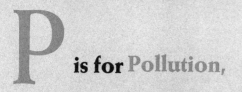

_____

when wastes are produced
faster than they can be
taken care of by natural
changes. Factories that give
off their wastes into lakes
and rivers pollute. Power
plants and automobiles that
give off poisonous gases into
the air pollute.

P is for photosynthesis,

_____

the process in green plants
that combines the carbon
dioxide of the air with water
to form sugar and starch.
Photosynthesis can only take
place in sunlight. Oxygen is
given off as a by-product. We
wouldn't have food to eat or
air to breathe without
photosynthesis.

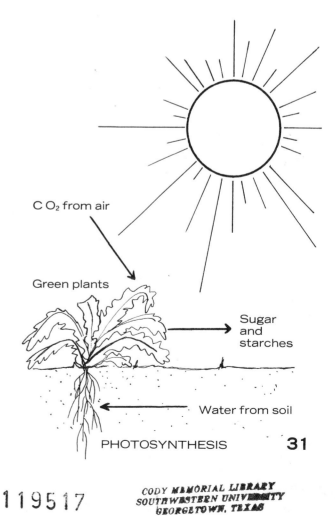

C O₂ from air

Green plants

Sugar
and
starches

Water from soil

PHOTOSYNTHESIS **31**

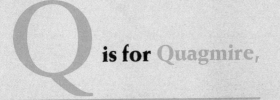

Q is for Quagmire,

soft, wet ground that your feet sink into. It might seem that quagmire ought to be dried out so that useful soil could be made out of it. Quagmire, however, is an important storage place for water. It is a kind of "wetland" that supports plants and animals important in the food chains of other animals.

Analyzing the exhaust gases from a test car

q is for quality criteria,

the standards people must meet in manufacturing
anything. It's a way of making sure that something
turned out by a factory is of good quality. Nowadays,
people must create new kinds of quality criteria that
will prevent manufacturing in a way that harms other
living things or pollutes the air and water.

33

R is for Radioactivity,

the way in which some atoms change into others. In doing so, they emit energy and very fast particles that can do harm to plants and animals. Men are using this energy from atomic power stations that produce radioactivity. They must be careful to keep this radioactivity from getting into the air, water, and soil.

Model of a nuclear power plant

save your
newspapers

save a tree

r is for recycling,

_____

_____

_____

using things over again. For example, this book is
made out of recycled paper. Trees were cut down and
used to make paper for a printing plant. The waste
paper from the printing plant was collected, treated,
and used to make paper for this book.

S is for Sewage,

_____

_____

_____

which is solid and liquid wastes. Water carries off the wastes and filth from homes, factories, and office buildings into rivers, lakes, and oceans. If too much is carried off, the rivers and lakes are changed so as to harm the living things in it. Germs can grow and spread disease. Sewage must be treated to make it less harmful before it enters natural waters.

S is for smog,

_____

_____

chemicals that combine with water to form a haze in the air. Smog irritates the lungs. If there is too much of it, it can damage the lungs and cause sickness. Most smog comes from the fuel burned by automobiles and incinerators.

T is for Topsoil,

the uppermost six inches of the soil. This contains most of the humus and is the most fertile part of the soil. It is turned over when land is plowed to make it easier for plants to grow. When lack of rain makes it dry up, the wind can blow some of it away or rain can wash it away. This makes the soil unusable for farming. Contour farming is used to keep the soil from washing away. The water collects in the furrows that follow the shape or **contour** of the hillside.

t is for tree,

_____

_____

a tall plant with a woody main stem. Many trees together make a forest. Trees serve as a home for many plants and animals. Their roots hold the soil together and keep it from washing away or blowing away. Men use the wood produced by trees in a thousand ways—from building houses to making paper.

U is for Ultraviolet radiation,

part of sunlight that is particularly full of energy. It is the ultraviolet radiation that causes sunburn. Ultraviolet radiation can be harmful to living things. There is a form of oxygen called ozone, high in the air, which blocks most of the ultraviolet and protects us all.

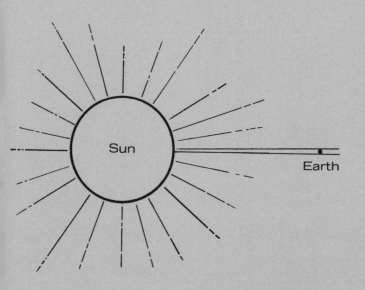

The earth receives only a small portion of the sun's ultraviolet radiation

Sun

Earth

U is for undergrowth,

the smaller plants that grow under and between the trees of a forest. These help make the forest an important place for many living things. Plants and animals find food and homes in the undergrowth. Some of the undergrowth is made up of young trees that grow up and replace the old trees when they die.

V is for Vegetation,

all the plant life of an area. The kind of vegetation present determines the kind of animals that can live in a region. Nothing can live that is not suited to the shade, moisture, and climate these plants provide. A great deal of vegetation means that many kinds of animals can live. When there is little water in an area, there is little vegetation. The result is a desert with fewer kinds of animals.

V is for vanishing species,

those species that are rapidly decreasing in numbers. With more and more people in the world, there is less and less room for other kinds of life. Some animals are killed by men. Some are accidentally poisoned. Some just don't have room to live. Tigers, orangutans, and cheetahs are examples of vanishing species.

CHEETAH

W is for Water cycle,

the passing of water from one place to another in nature. Water evaporates from oceans and lakes because of the sun's heat. The water vapor forms clouds in the air. The clouds send water down to the earth as rain. The rain soaks into the ground, flows into the rivers and back into the oceans and lakes.

42

W is for weather,

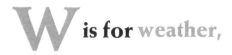

the changing conditions of the air. The air changes in its temperature, in the amount of water vapor it has, in the speed with which it is moving. It can be windy, rainy, snowy, foggy, cold, or hot. Every place on earth has its own kind of weather.

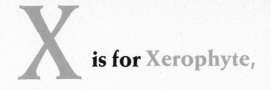

X is for Xerophyte,

_____

_____

_____

any plant that can grow in a dry place and get along with little water. Such plants have long roots that go deep into the ground to reach water. Or they have roots spread out over a wide area. These plants may have no leaves at all, or the leaves may be very small in size. This keeps them from losing too much water by evaporation. Many xerophytes, like cactus, also store water in their stems.

X is for xylophage,

_____

_____

_____

a living thing that feeds on wood. Wood-eating is
important because otherwise wood would pile up as
trees die, and the earth would be cluttered with it.
Termites and certain beetles are examples of
xylophages.

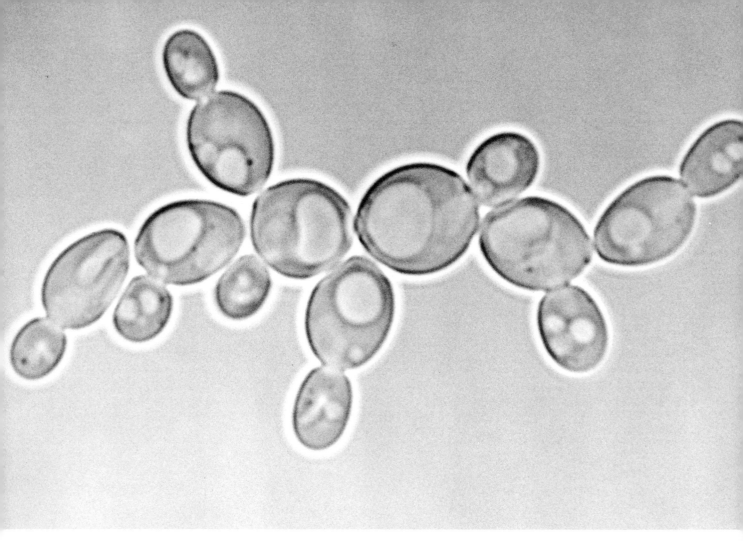

Y is for Yeast,

tiny one-celled plants that feed on sugar. Yeast gives off two waste products. One is alcohol and the other is the gas, carbon dioxide. Sometimes the alcohol by-product is important, as when yeast changes malt sugar into beer and grape sugar into wine. Sometimes, the carbon dioxide is important, as when yeast acts on the sugar in bread and carbon dioxide accumulates in the dough and makes it rise.

 **is for** yield,

_____

_____

_____

the quantity of a particular living thing that can be taken and used by people without harming the surroundings. A certain number of trees can be taken out of a forest and new trees will grow to replace them. But if too many trees are taken, the forest will thin out and there will be fewer trees later on. The yield will decrease.

47

Z is for Zoology,

_____

_____

_____

the study of animals. People
must consider the structure
and functions of animals
in order to understand their
relationship to their
environment.

Z is for zonation,

_____

_____

_____

the division of any part of the
land or sea into a series of
places in which different
animals and plants live. The
ocean can be divided into
zones at different depths,
where there is less and less
light. A mountain side can
be divided into zones at
different heights, where it
gets colder and colder. As
you go up, the vegetation
changes.